C++

A Step-by-Step Guide for Absolute Beginners

Daniel BELL

GUZZLER
MEDIA

C++: A Step-by-Step Guide For Absolute Beginners

Publisher: Guzzler Media LLC

http://www.guzzlermedia.com
Contact: contact@guzzlermedia.com
Book and Cover design by Angela W.T.
ISBN: 9781694606686
Imprint: Independently published
First Edition: July 2019

CONTENTS

"C++: Where friends have access to your private members."

Gavin Russell Baker

Introduction

C++ is one of the popular computer programming languages. This can be attributed to the fact that C++ comes fully-packed with great features that are good for the development of great computer applications. C++ has both low-level and high-level computer programming features. With the low-level features offered by C++, software developers and computer programmers are able to create applications that are close to the computer hardware. These are applications that can communicate directly with the computer hardware. A good example of such applications is device drivers such as the Bluetooth driver of your computer. The high-level features offered by C++ are good for the development of software applications that are close to the end users. These are the applications that users directly interact with. A good example of such an application is a text editor.

C++ is an object-oriented programming language. This

marks the greatest difference between C and C++ programming languages. The object-oriented allows the development of better applications. It also makes programming easy, especially for beginners. You can quickly get started with C++, because you only need basic components for this, and they are open sources. That is why; C++ is one of the best languages for computer programming for beginners. This tutorial is an excellent guide to learn C++. All features provided by C++ have been discussed.

1-Getting Started with C++

An Overview of C++

C++ is a compiled object-oriented programming language. It is well-known for combining both low-level and high-level programming language features, making it a middle-level programming language.

Bjarne Stroustrup began to develop C++ in **1979** at Bell Labs Murray Hill, New Jersey. The language was meant to be an enhancement to the C programming language and hence given the name C with Classes. In 1983, the language was named C++. This shows that C++ is a superset of C and any C program is a legal C++ program.

Since C++ is an object-oriented programming language, it

offers us with the following object-oriented programming features:

- Encapsulation
- Inheritance
- Data hiding
- Polymorphism

C++ is used widely by programmers developing different kinds of applications. It has been used widely for development of device drivers and other applications that manipulate the hardware directly in real-time constraints. It is also used widely used for research and academic purposes since its concepts are good for teaching.

Environment Setup

To write and run a C++ program, you only need a text editor and the C++ compiler.

The text editor will provide you with an environment where you will type the program. Some of the text editors that you can use include **Windows Notepad, Brief, Epsilon, EMACS, OS Edit command**, and **vim/vi**.

The names and versions of the various text editors will normally different in various operating system environments. The Notepad text editor, for example, can only be used on the Windows operating system while vim can be used on both Windows and Unix operating systems.

After writing your code in a file, the file will be referred to as the *source file* and its name should end with a **.cpp**, **.p** or **.c** extension. Ensure that your computer is installed with a text editor for writing your C++ programs.

The purpose of the C++ compiler is to compile your C++ source file into an executable program. Majority of the C++ compilers have no problem with the kind of extension that you give to your source file, but by default, the compiler will use the .cpp extension. The most popular of all the C++ compilers is the GNU C/C++ compiler **(GCC).** There are also compilers from Solaris and HP for those running their operating systems.

For Linux and Unix users, your system comes installed with the GCC, so you can check the installed version by running the following command:

g++ -v

If gcc is already installed on your system, you will be able to see its version. If not, you will have to install it yourself by following the detailed instructions that you can find on the following web page:

https://gcc.gnu.org/install/

For MAC OS X users, you can get **gcc** by installing the XCode development environment which you can find from the official Apple's website. You can then follow the necessary instructions to install it.

To get the gcc on Windows, you can install the **MinGW**. You can find it on its official web page given below:

http://www.mingw.org/

After the download, install and setup the path environment variable so that you can have no problem while trying to compile your C++ source files.

2-C++ Program Structure

A C++ program can be seen as a collection of objects that communicate with each other through invoking the methods of each other. Let us define some terms that we will be using throughout this book to describe various parts of our programs:

- **Object-** an object has both state and behaviors. For example, a car is an object with properties such as color, capacity, etc. Examples of its behaviors include accelerating, stopping, etc. See an object as an instance of a class.

- **Class-** a class is a blueprint describing the states and behaviors that objects of its type should exhibit.

- **Methods-** A method is simply a behavior. A class may have numerous methods. Logics are written within these methods, actions are executed and data are manipulated.

- **Instance Variables-** every object comes with a unique set of instance variables. The state of an object is created by the values that are assigned to these instance variables.

Consider the simple C++ program given below:

```cpp
#include <iostream>
using namespace std;
// main() marks where the program execution
begins.
int main() {
    cout << "Hello World!"; // to print Hello
World!
    return 0;
}
```

Let us discuss the various parts of the above program:

- **# include <iostream>-** Any C++ line that begins with a **#** is a directive that will be read and interpreted by what is called the ***preprocessor.*** Such lines are special and have to be interpreted before the entire program is compiled.

  The **<iostream>** is a header. C++ language provides us with numerous headers that store information that we may need when writing and running our programs. In the **<iostream>** header, there is a lot of information that has been defined for us to use. Instead of defining this information from scratch, we only have to call this header and access this information for free. It defines how standard input and output operations are done, such as printing the output of this program on the screen.

- using namespace **std;**- This line instructs the C++ compiler to make use of the std namespace. **N**amspaces were added recently to the C++ language.
- // **main()** marks where the program execution begins.- this whole line is a comment. It only helps in making the program readable by humans. The C++ compiler will skip or ignore this line. The use of // at its beginning marked the line as a comment. If the comment spanned multiple lines, we could have enclosed it within /* and */.
- **int main() {**- this is the main method and marks where the execution of the program begins. The opening curly brace { marks the beginning of the body of this method.
- **cout << "Hello World!"; //** to print Hello World!- the purpose of this line is to print the message *Hello World!* on the screen. The *cout* is a function that has been defined in the **<iostream>** header file. Our work is to simply call this function and pass the text that should be printed to it. It stands for *console output*. The rest of the line from // will be treated as a comment, hence the C++ compiler will skip it.
- **return 0;**- the purpose of this line is to terminate the main function. It will also cause it to return a value of 0 to the calling process.

}- the closing curly brace marks the end of the **main()** **method** body.

Compiling and Executing C++ Programs

To see the output from the above program, you have to compile and execute it. Follow the steps given below:

- Opening your text editor and type the above code into it.
- Save the file with the name *hello.cpp.*
- Launch the command prompt of your operating system and navigate to the directory in which you have saved the above file.
- Type the command *g++ hello.cpp* and hit the enter key on your keyboard. If your code has no errors, the **a.out** file will be generated and you will be taken to the next line.
- Now, execute the program by typing *a.out* on the command prompt and hit the enter key.

The text *Hello World!* will be printed on the screen.

```
$ g++ hello.cpp
$ ./a.out
```

3-C++ Data Types

When programming in C++, we will need a way of storing data into the memory. This can be done by use of variables. Variables help us reserve memory spaces for storage of values. This means that every time that a variable is created, some space is reserved in the memory.

Variables belong to different data types. The data type determines the type of data, whether a *string* or *numeric* etc. that you can store in the reserved memory location as well as the amount of space that is reserved for that variable in the computer memory.

In C++, data types are put into different categories. Let us discuss these:

Primitive Built-in Types

C++ provides us with numerous built-in as well as user-defined data types. The following are the common data types and the amount of memory space allocated to them:

- **char-** has a storage size of 1 byte.
- **int-** has a storage size of 4 bytes.
- **float-** has a storage size of 4 bytes.
- **double-** has a storage size of 8 bytes.

Note that above are just samples of the data types available in C++. To see the size of each of these data types, you can use the *sizeof()* **operator**. The following C++ program demonstrates how to use this operator:

```
#include <iostream>
using namespace std;
int main() {
    cout << "char has a size of : " <<
sizeof(char) << endl;
    cout << "int has a size of : " << sizeof(int)
<< endl;
    cout << "short int has a size of : " <<
sizeof(short int) << endl;
    cout << "long int has a size of : " <<
sizeof(long int) << endl;
    cout << "float has a size of : " <<
sizeof(float) << endl;
    cout << "double has a size of : " <<
sizeof(double) << endl;
    cout << "wchar_t has a size of : " <<
sizeof(wchar_t) << endl;

    return 0;
}
```

When executed, it should print the following:

```
char has a size of : 1
int has a size of : 4
short int has a size of : 2
long int has a size of : 8
float has a size of : 4
double has a size of : 8
wchar_t has a size of : 4
```

What we have done is that we have called the *sizeof()* operator and passed to it the names of different data types. It then returned to us the sizes of these various data types. The text enclosed within double quotes will be printed as it is on the console. Notice the use of the *endl* statement, which inserts a new line character at the end of every line. This means that printing will start on the next line.

`typedef` Declarations

A new name can be created for an already existing type by use of the *typedef* operator. This keyword should be used with the following syntax:

`typedef` type new_name;

For example, to give the **int data** type the name *myint,* we can run the following command:

`typedef` int myint;

After running the above command, the following will be a valid declaration:

myint distance;

We will have created an **int type** variable named *distance*.

4 - C + +
Variables

The purpose of variables is to create named storages for our programs to manipulate. Each variable in C++ belongs to a certain data type which determines the amount of memory size allocated to the variable and the kind of data that the variable can hold. It also determines the range of values that can be stored within that memory space as well as the operations that we can apply to it.

Variables are given names. The name of a variable can be made up of characters, digits and the underscore (_). However, the name must begin with either a letter or an underscore, otherwise, an error will be generated. Note that C++ is a case sensitive programming language, hence, it distinguishes between lowercase and uppercase letters. This means that you have to refer to values correctly by their exact names. Whitespace is allowed in a variable name. A variable name must also not be any of the reserved keywords in C++.

Variable Definition

A variable definition is the processing of telling the C++ compiler where and the amount of memory size to allocate to a certain variable. The definition of a variable is made up of a data type and the name of names of variables. This means that more than one variable can be defined within a single line. It should be done by following the syntax given below:

```
type variable_list;
```

In the above syntax, the type must be a valid C++ data type such as **char, int, float double,** etc. The variable list is the list of variable names that are to be defined and these should be separated by commas. The following are valid examples of variable definitions:

```
int a, b, z;
char    c, ch;
float   f, wage;
double d;
```

The **int a, b, z;** defines three variables names a, b and z in a single line and they all belong to the same data type.

Assignment of values to the variables can be done at the time of variable definition. The assignment can be done using the equal (=) sign followed by a constant expression.

The following syntax demonstrates this:

```
type variable_name = variable_value;
```

The following examples demonstrate this:

```
int a = 3, b = 5;              // definition and
initializing a and b.
byte p = 20;                   // definition and
initializes p.
char c = 'c';                  // the variable c has
the value 'c'.
```

Variable Declaration

The purpose of a variable declaration is to provide the compiler with the assurance that there exists only one variable that is existing with that given type and name for the compiler to continue with further compilation without having to require complete details regarding the variable.

Variable declaration becomes very important when you have defined more than one files and the variable has been defined in one of the files, so it becomes very useful at the time when the two files are to be linked. You can use the *extern* keyword for you to declare a variable at any place.

A variable can be declared many times within a C++ program, but you can only define it once within a file function or block of code.

In the example given below, we have declared a variable at the top but its definition has been done inside the main function:

```cpp
#include <iostream>
using namespace std;
// Variable declaration:
extern int x, y;
extern int z;
extern float f;

int main () {
    // Variable definition:
    int x, y;
    int z;
    float f;

    // actual initialization
    x = 5;
    y = 12;
    z = x + y;

    cout << z << endl ;

    f = 45.0/2.0;
    cout << f << endl ;

    return 0;
}
```

The code should return the following output upon execution:

```
17
22.5
```

This concept is also applied in a **function declaration** in which the function name is provided during the time of declaration but the real definition is done anywhere else.

The following example demonstrates this:

```cpp
// function declaration
int myfunc();
```

```
int main() {
    // function call
    int x = myfunc();
}
// function definition
int myfunc() {
    return 0;
}
```

Variable Scope

A scope refers to a region or place within a program. In C++, there are **3 scopes** in which we can declare our variables:

Inside a block or a function leading to a *local variable.*

In the definition of the parameters of a function leading to *formal parameters.*

Outside all functions leading to a *global variable.*

Let us discuss the difference between local and global variables:

Local Variables

These are the types of variables that have been defined inside a block of code or inside a function. Such variables can only be accessed from within the block or function where they have been defined. This means that only those statements within that block of function can access the variable. The variable cannot be accessed from within other functions. The following example demonstrates the concept of local variables in C++:

```
#include <iostream>
using namespace std;
int main () {
    // declaration of a Local variable
    int x, y;
    int z;
    // actual initialization
    x = 5;
    y = 12;
    z = x + y;

    cout <<"The value of z is "<<z;

    return 0;
}
```

All variables, that is, x, y, and z have been defined within the *main()* function. We have also accessed these values from within that function. They are all local variables. The code should return the following result upon execution:

```
The value of z is 17
```

Global Variables

These are functions that are defined outside all functions, and most probably at the top of the program. A global variable will hold value throughout the whole life of a program.

Any function within the program can access the global variable. This means that a global variable will be available for access throughout the whole life of the program after its declaration. The example given below demonstrates the use of

Daniel Bell

both local and global variables:

```
#include <iostream>
using namespace std;

// Declaration of a global variable
int g;

int main () {
    // Local variable declaration:
    int x, y;

    // actual initialization
    x = 12;
    y = 5;
    g = x + y;

    cout <<"The value of the global variable g is "<<g;

    return 0;
}
```

Notice the declaration of the variable g. It has been done outside the **main() function**, making it a global variable. This variable can be accessed from any function defined within our code. We have then accessed this variable from within the **main() function** although it has been defined outside it. The code should return the following result, showing that the variable was accessed successfully:

```
The value of the global variable g is 17
```

It is possible for us to have the same name for a local and a global variable. However, the value assigned to the local variable will take preference. This means that when we try to access the value of the variable, the value assigned to the local variable one will be returned first. The following example demonstrates this:

```cpp
#include <iostream>
using namespace std;

// Declaration of a global variable
int g = 5;

int main () {
    // Declaration of a local variable
    int g = 12;

    cout <<"The value of variable g is "<<g;

    return 0;
}
```

In the above example, we have declared the same variable twice, that is, the variable g. In the first declaration, g is a global variable since it has been declared outside the *main()* **function.** We have assigned it a value of 5. In the second declaration, g has been declared within the *main()* **function** and assigned a value of 12, making it a local variable. We have then tried to access the value of this variable. The code returns the following:

```
The value of variable g is 12
```

The above output shows that the value of variable g assigned to the local version has been given priority.

5 - C++ Constants

Constants are fixed values that programs may not be allowed to alter and they are referred to as *literals*. A constant can belong to any of the available basic data types. Note that are just regular variables with the difference being that the values of constants cannot be changed after definition.

C++ provides us with two ways of defining constants. These include the following:

- Using the *#define* preprocessor.
- Using the *const* keyword.

Let us discuss how to use these two:

To define a constant using the **#define preprocessor**, we use the syntax given below:

```
#define identifier value
```

The *identifier* is the name of the name of the constant while the *value* denotes the value assigned to the constant. The following program describes how this can be done:

```cpp
#include <iostream>
using namespace std;

#define WIDTH   7
#define LENGTH 11

int main() {
    int rectangle_area;

    rectangle_area = LENGTH * WIDTH;
    cout <<"The area of the rectangle is
"<<rectangle_area;
    return 0;
}
```

In the above example, we have defined two constants namely **WIDTH** and **LENGTH**. We have assigned values of **7** and **11** to these respectively. We have also defined the variable *rectangle_area* and assigned it the value of the product of the two constants. We have then printed out the value of this variable.

When executed, the code should return the following as the output:

```
The area of the rectangle is 77
```

Using the const Keyword

We can also define a constant by use of the ***const*** keyword. To do this, we have to use the syntax given below:

```
const data_type variable = value;
```

Note that we have to define the data type of the constant. The value of the constant this time has been assigned using the assignment (=) operator. Let us give an example demonstrating this:

```cpp
#include <iostream>
using namespace std;

int main() {
    const int  LENGTH = 7;
    const int  WIDTH  = 11;
    int rectangle_area;

    rectangle_area = LENGTH * WIDTH;
    cout <<"The area of the rectangle is "<<
rectangle_area;
    return 0;
}
```

We have just created the same example but this time, the constants have been defined using the const keyword.

When executed, the code should return the following result:

```
The area of the rectangle is 77
```

Note that programmatically, it is always good to name constants in upper case.

6 - C++ Operators

An operator refers to a symbol used for performing operations. C++ comes with different operators for performing different kinds of operations. These operators have been grouped into the following categories:

- Arithmetic Operators
- Relational Operators
- Logical Operators

Let us discuss these types of operators one by one.

Arithmetic Operators

These are the operators used for performing basic math operations such as addition, multiplication, subtraction, division, etc. Let us create an example that demonstrates how to use these operators in C++:

```cpp
#include <iostream>
using namespace std;

main() {
    int x = 7;
    int y = 5;
    int z ;

    z = x + y;
    cout << "x + y is " << z << endl ;

    z = x - y;
    cout << "x - y is  :" << z << endl
    ;
    z = x * y;
    cout << "x * y is " << z << endl ;

    z = x / y;
    cout << "x / y is " << z << endl ;

    z = x % y;
    cout << "x % y is " << z << endl ;

    z = x++;
    cout << "x++ is " << z << endl ;

    z = x--;
    cout << "x-- is " << z << endl ;

    return 0;
}
```

When executed, the code should print the following result:

```
x + y is 12
x - y is  :2
x * y is 35
x / y is 1
x % y is 2
x++ is 7
x-- is 8
```

We began by defining three variables namely **x, y,** and **z.** Variables **x** and **y** have been assigned the values **7** and **5** respectively.

The expression **z = x + y**; calculates the sum of the values of variables x and y and assigns the result to variable **z.** That is why it returns **12.**

The expression **z = x - y**; subtracts the value of variable y from the value of variable x and assigns the result to variable **z.** That is it returns **2.**

The expression **z = x * y**; calculates the product of the values of variables **x** and **y** and assigns the result to variable **z.** That is it returns **35.**

The expression **z = x / y**; calculates the division of the value of variable **x** by the value of variable y and assigns the result to variable **z.** That is why it returns **1.** Note that the decimal part has been ignored since our variables are integers rather than float values.

The expression **z = x % y**; calculates the remainder after dividing the value of variable **x** by the value of the variable and assigns the result to variable **z.** That is it returns **2.** The **%** is known as the modulus operator.

The expression **z = x ++**; increments the value of variable **x** by 1 and assigns the result to variable **z.** That is it returns **7.** However, the value of the variable **x** has not changed. This is because it accesses it when it still **7** and prints. However, the value is changed to **8** and it will affect the next expression.

The expression **z = x --**; decrements the value of variable x by **1** and assigns the result to variable **z.** That is it returns **8.** Note that the value had been incremented in the previous operation. The answer is **8** because it accesses it when it still **8** and prints.

Relational Operators

These operators help us check the relationship between various variables in a program. They include the following:

- == will return true if both left and right sides are equal.
- != will return true if left and right sides of the operator are not equal.
- \> returns true if the left side is greater than the right side.
- < returns true if the left side is less than the right side.
- \>= returns true if left side is greater than/equal to right.
- <= returns true if the left side is less than the right side.

The following example demonstrates how to use these operators:

```
#include <iostream>
using namespace std;

main() {
    int x = 11;
    int y = 8;
    int z ;

    cout << "For x= 11 and y=8:"<< endl;

    if( x == y ) {
        cout << "x == y is true" << endl ;
    } else {
        cout << "x == y is false" << endl ;
    }
```

```cpp
if( x < y ) {
    cout << "x < y is true" << endl ;
} else {
    cout << "x < y is false" << endl ;
}

if( x > y ) {
    cout << "x > y is true" << endl ;
} else {
    cout << "x > y is false" << endl ;
}

/* Let's change the values of a and b */
cout << "For x= 4 and y=12:"<< endl;
x = 4;
y = 12;
if( x <= y ) {
    cout << "x <= y is true" << endl ;
}

if( y >= x ) {
    cout << "y >= x is true" << endl ;
}

return 0;
}
```

The code returns the following output upon execution:

```
For x= 11 and y=8:
x == y is false
x < y is false
x > y is true
For x= 4 and y=12:
x <= y is true
y >= x is true
```

Note that we began by the values of x as **11** and y as **8**. We have then changed these values to **x=4** and **y=12**.

Logical Operators

C++ supports the following logical operators:

a1&&a2- called the logical **AND**. Will return **true** if both **a1** and **a2** are **true**, otherwise, **false**.

a1||a2- called the logical **OR**. Will return false if both **a1** and **a2** are **false**, otherwise **true**.

!a1- called logical **NOT**. Will return opposite of **a1**.

The following example demonstrates how to use the above operators:

```cpp
#include <iostream>
using namespace std;

main() {
    int x = 10;
    int y = 25;
    int z ;

    cout<< "For x=10 and y=25:"<< endl;

    if(x && y) {
        cout << "x && y is true"<< endl ;
    }

    if(x || y) {
        cout << "x || y is true"<< endl ;
    }

    /* change values of  x and y */
    x = 0;
    y = 5;

    cout<< "For x=0 and y=5"<< endl;

    if(x && y) {
        cout << "x && y is true"<< endl ;
    } else {
```

```
    cout << "x && y is not true"<< endl ;
}

if(!(x && y)) {
    cout << "!(x && y) is true"<< endl ;
}

return 0;
}
```

The code prints the following result:

```
For x=10 and y=25:
x && y is true
x || y is true
For x=0 and y=5
x && y is not true
!(x && y) is true
```

Operator Precedence

Operator precedence determines the way the terms of expression are grouped. This has a great impact on the expression and the final result it gives. Some operators have higher precedence than others. For example, the multiplication operator has higher precedence compared to the addition operator.

Consider the following math expression:

```
x = 4 + 5 * 2;
```

The variable **x** will be assigned a value of **14,** not **18**. This is because ***** is given higher precedence than the **+** operator. The multiplication operation will be done first, that is, **5 * 2** to give

10 and then **4** will be added to it.

Consider the following postfix operators:

```
() [] -> . ++ - -
```

Their order of decreasing precedence runs from left to right, meaning that the () operator is given the highest precedence followed by [], etc.

Here is another set of unary operators:

```
+ - ! ~ ++ - - (type)* & sizeof
```

Their order of decreasing precedence runs from right to left, meaning that the *sizeof* operator is given the highest precedence followed by **&,** etc.

Here is a set of multiplicative operators:

```
* / %
```

Their order of decreasing precedence runs from right to left, meaning that the ***** operator is given the highest precedence followed by **/** etc.

The following C++ program demonstrates the concept of operator precedence:

```
#include <iostream>
using namespace std;

main() {
    int x = 20;
    int y = 10;
    int z = 15;
    int d = 5;
    int ans;
```

```
    ans = (x + y) * z / d;        // ( 30 * 15 ) / 5
    cout << "Value of (x + y) * z / d is :" << ans
<< endl ;

    ans = ((x + y) * z) / d;      // (30 * 15 ) / 5
    cout << "Value of ((a + b) * c) / d is   :" <<
ans << endl ;

    ans = (x + y) * (z / d);      // (30) * (15/5)
    cout << "Value of (a + b) * (c / d) is   :" <<
ans << endl ;

    ans = x + (y * z) / d;        //  20 + (150/5)
    cout << "Value of x + (y * z) / d is   :" <<
ans << endl ;

    return 0;
}
```

The comments make it easy for you to understand how the operations have been performed. When you execute the code, it should return the following result:

```
Value of (x + y) * z / d is :90
Value of ((a + b) * c) / d is   :90
Value of (a + b) * (c / d) is   :90
Value of x + (y * z) / d is   :50
```

In all expressions, the operation placed within the () has been given the highest precedence, hence, it was evaluated first.

7 - C + + Loops

Loops provide us with an automated way of performing certain tasks repetitively. This is the case when we need to execute part of our code repeatedly. The statements of code placed within a loop are executed sequentially, that is, in the order that you have written them.

There are different types of loops that we can create in C++. Let us discuss these:

while Loop

A *while* **loop** is very simple. You state a condition and the block of statements will only be executed when the loop condition is true. This means that the loop condition is evaluated first before executing the block of statements. If the condition is found to be true, then the block of statements is executed.

What is the condition evaluates to a false? The block of statements will not be executed but it will be skipped. This means that a while loop may never run. The while loop takes the following syntax:

```
while(condition) {
    statement(s);
}
```

In the above syntax, we can have a single statement or a sequence of statements. The loop body placed between { and } will be iterated as long as the condition is true. When the condition becomes false, the statements within the loop body will be skipped. The following program demonstrates the use of a *while* loop:

```
#include <iostream>
using namespace std;

int main () {
    // Declaration of a local variable
    int x = 5;

    // while loop execution
    while( x <= 10 ) {
        cout << "value of x is: " << x << endl;
        x++;
    }

    return 0;
}
```

In the above example, we have declared a local variable named x and assigned it a value of **5**. Our goal is to increment this by **1** after each iteration of the while loop.

Consider the following expression extracted from the code:

```
while( x <= 10 )
```

The above expression means that as long as the value of variable **x** is less than or equal to **10**, the loop body should be executed. This means that for values between **5** and **10**, the loop condition will evaluate to a true. When the value of **x** becomes **11**, the loop condition will evaluate to a false, hence the execution of the loop body will stop. That is why the code returns the following result upon execution:

```
value of x is: 5
value of x is: 6
value of x is: 7
value of x is: 8
value of x is: 9
value of x is: 10
```

We stated that the while loop may never run. Let us change the initial value of variable **x** to **11** and see what will happen:

```
#include <iostream>
using namespace std;
int main () {
   // Declaration of a local variable
   int x = 11;

   // while loop execution
   while( x <= 10 ) {
      cout << "value of x is: " << x << endl;
      x++;
   }
   return 0;
}
```

The above code will return nothing upon execution. The reason is that the loop condition will evaluate to a false on its first evaluation, hence, its body will not be executed.

for Loop

This type of loop is very good and efficient when you know the exact number of times that you need to repeat a task. The loop takes the following syntax:

```
for ( initial; condition; increment ) {
    statement(s);
}
```

The *initial* part of the loop allows you to declare and initialize the variable that you will use to control the execution of the loop. In our case, this is the variable **x**. We can set it to **x=5**.

The *condition* part is where you specify the condition that must be true for the loop body to be executed. In our case, this is where we specify that the value of variable **x** should be less than or equal to **10**. We can set this to **x<=10**.

The *increment* is where the flow will jump after each iteration. It specifies how we should modify the loop control variable after every iteration. This is where we add the **x++** statement to increment the variable by **1** after every iteration.

The compiler will evaluate the condition after every iteration to check whether it is **true** or **false**. If true, it will jump to the increment part then the loop body. This is repeated until the condition becomes **false**.

Here is an example:

Daniel Bell

```
#include <iostream>
using namespace std;
int main () {
// Declaration of a local variable
    int x;
        // for loop execution
    for(x=5;x<=10;x++) {
        cout << "value of x is: " << x << endl;
    }

    return 0;
}
```

The code will return the following result upon execution:

```
value of x is: 5
value of x is: 6
value of x is: 7
value of x is: 8
value of x is: 9
value of x is: 10
```

Notice that just like the *while* loop, the *for* loop may never execute. This is the case when we set the initial value of the control variable to a value that violates the condition. For example:

```
#include <iostream>
using namespace std;

int main () {
    // Declaration of a local variable
    int x;

    // for loop execution
    for(x=11;x<=10;x++) {
        cout << "value of x is: " << x << endl;
    }
```

```
    return 0;
}
```

The value of variable **x** has been set to **11**, while the loop condition checks whether it is less than or equal to **10**. The loop condition will evaluate into false upon the first evaluation, hence, the loop body will never be executed. This means that the code returns nothing when executed.

do ... while Loop

In the ***while*** and ***for*** loops, we were evaluating the loop control condition at the top of the loop body. This is why in some cases; the loop body was never executed.

This is different from the ***do...while*** loop. The loop control condition is evaluated at the end of the loop body. This means that the loop body must be evaluated for at least once, even when the condition evaluates to a false for the first time. This type of loop takes the following syntax:

```
do {
    statement(s);
}
while( condition );
```

After the first iteration, when the condition evaluates to a true, control will jump back to the do part. If it evaluates to a false, the execution will continue downwards without going back to the loop. This means that as long as the condition is true, the loop body will keep on executing. Let us create an example that demonstrates this:

Daniel Bell

```
#include <iostream>
using namespace std;

int main () {
    // Declaration of a local variable
    int x = 5;

    // do loop execution
    do {
        cout << "value of x is: " << x << endl;
            x++;

    }
    while (x<=10);
      return 0;
}
```

When executed, the code will return the following:

```
value of x is: 5
value of x is: 6
value of x is: 7
value of x is: 8
value of x is: 9
value of x is: 10
```

The value of variable **x** was initialized to **5**. The compiler will pass through the loop body for the first time and return **5** for the value of **x**. It will encounter the increment, **x++,** and increment this value to a **6**. When it reaches the loop condition, **x<=10**, it will find that the condition is true. It will jump back to the do part and execute the loop body. The value of **x** will be incremented to **7** and the loop condition will still be true. Again, it will jump to the do part. This will be done a couple of times until when the value of **x** is found to be **11**. This time, the

loop condition will evaluate to a false and it won't jump back to
the do part. The execution of the loop will halt.

Nested for Loop

We get a nested *for* loop when we add a *for* loop inside
another *for* loop. For a single iteration of the outer loop, the
inner loop will be executed fully. This means that if the outer
loop is executed for **4** times, the inner loop will be **4** times for
each, meaning that it will be executed for **16** times. Here is an
example:

```cpp
#include <iostream>
using namespace std;

int main () {
        for(int x=1;x<=3;x++){
            for(int y=1;y<=3;y++){
            cout<<x<<" "<<y<<"\n";
        }
        }
    }
```

The variable **x** has been declared in the outer loop while
the variable **y** has been declared in the inner loop.

For each value of **x**, the **y** should be returned **3** times as
shown in the following output:

```
1 1
1 2
1 3
2 1
2 2
2 3
3 1
3 2
3 3
```

At this point, you should be conversant with using different types of loops in **C++**. These statements are known as *loop control statements* and they change the execution of a loop from the normal to something else. Let us discuss the various loop control statements supported in **C++**:

break Statement

The purpose of this statement is to break the loop at a specified condition. When the C++ compiler encounters this statement, it halts the execution of the loop and jumps to the statements that come after the loop.

If you use the ***break*** statement inside an inner loop, it will stop the execution of the inner loop and the line that comes after the block will be executed. The following example demonstrates the use of the ***break*** statement in C++:

```cpp
#include <iostream>
using namespace std;
int main() {
    for (int x = 5; x <= 10; x++)
    {
        if (x == 8)
```

```
                {
                    break;
                }
            cout<<"The value of x is: " <<x<<endl;
            }
}
```

When you execute the code, it should return the following:

```
The value of x is: 5
The value of x is: 6
The value of x is: 7
```

The reason for the above output is that we created a **break** for when the value of variable **x** is **8**. When it reached **8**, the execution of the loop halted.

continue Statement

This statement helps us to *continue* a loop. It causes the execution of the loop to be resumed, and any code in between is ignored or skipped. Here is an example:

```
#include <iostream>
using namespace std;
int main() {
        for (int x = 5; x <= 10; x++)
            {
                if (x == 8)
                {
                  continue;
                }
```

```
        cout<<"The value of x is: " <<x<<endl;
            }
    }
```

The code will return the following result:

```
The value of x is: 5
The value of x is: 6
The value of x is: 7
The value of x is: 9
The value of x is: 10
```

There is no value for **x** equals **8**. However, instead of halting the execution of the loop, it continues from there and prints the values for **9** and **10**. That is how different the *continue* statement is different from the *break* statement.

goto Statement

It is also called the *jump* statement. We use it when we need to transfer control to another part of the program. It will jump unconditionally to the specified label. Consider the following example:

```
#include <iostream>
using namespace std;

int main () {
    // Declaring a local variable:
    int x = 5;

    // do loop execution
```

```
LOOP:do {
    if( x == 8) {
        // skip the iteration.
        x = x + 1;
        goto LOOP;
    }
    cout << "value of x is: " << x << endl;
    x = x + 1;
}
while( x <= 10 );

return 0;
}
```

It should return the following result:

```
value of x is: 5
value of x is: 6
value of x is: 7
value of x is: 9
value of x is: 10
```

8-Decision Making

Decision making in programming simply involves setting a number of conditions that are to be evaluated alongside the statements to be executed when the various conditions are true. Optionally, the programmer can set the statements to be executed when the conditions are not true.

There are various C++ statements that we can use to make decisions in C++. Let us discuss them:

if Statement

To create an *if* statement, we define a Boolean expression which is then followed by either one or more statements.

This is demonstrated by the following syntax:

```
if(expression) {
    // statement(s)
}
```

The statement(s) will only be executed if the Boolean expression is true. If not true, nothing will be done. In such a case, execution will jump to the section of the code that comes after the *if* body. The following code demonstrates this:

```cpp
#include <iostream>
using namespace std;

int main () {
    // Declaration of a local variable:
    int x = 5;

    // check the boolean condition
    if( x < 10 ) {
        // if condition is true then print the
following
        cout << "Variable x is less than 10" <<
endl;
    }
    cout << "Variable x is : " << x << endl;

    return 0;
}
```

The co0de should return the following output:

```
Variable x is less than 10
Variable x is : 5
```

We created a local variable **x** and assigned it a value of **5**. In the Boolean expression, we are checking whether this value is less than 10. Since this is true, the statement within the body of the *if* was executed. The part outside the *if* was also executed because it will always be executed, whether the expression is true or false.

Now, let us change the value of **x** to **20** for the Boolean expression to become false:

```cpp
#include <iostream>
using namespace std;

int main () {
   // Declaration of a local variable:
   int x = 20;

   // check the boolean condition
   if( x < 10 ) {
      // if condition is true then print the
following
      cout << "Variable x is less than 10" <<
endl;
   }
   cout << "Variable x is : " << x << endl;

   return 0;
}
```

We have x equals to **20**. In the Boolean expression, we are checking whether this value is less than **10**. The Boolean expression evaluates to a false, hence the statement inside the body of *if* will not be executed. This means that only the part outside the if body will be executed to return the following result:

```
Variable x is : 20
```

if... else Statement

We use this statement when we need to specify the part that will be executed when the *if* condition evaluates to a false. This is specified within the *else* part. The statement takes the syntax given below:

```
if(expression) {
    // statement(s) to be executed if the boolean
expression is true
} else {
    // statement(s) to be executed if the boolean
expression is false
}
```

The following example demonstrates this:

```
#include <iostream>
using namespace std;
int main () {
    int x = 15;
            if (x % 2 == 0)
            {
                cout<<"X is an even number";
            }
            else
            {
                cout<<"X is an odd number";
            }
    return 0;
}
```

We have created the variable **x** and assigned it a value of **15**. In our, *if* Boolean expression, we are checking whether we remain with **0** after dividing **x** by **2**, that is, we are checking whether **x** is an even number. This is false since we remain with **1** after dividing **15** by **2**.

This means that the statement within the body of the *if* will be skipped and the else part will be executed to return the following result:

```
X is an odd number
```

Now, let us change the value of variable **x** from **15** to **20** and see the result that we get:

```cpp
#include <iostream>
using namespace std;
int main () {
    int x = 20;
            if (x % 2 == 0)
            {
                    cout<<"X is an even number";
            }
            else
            {
                    cout<<"X is an odd number";
            }
    return 0;
}
```

The code returns the following:

```
X is an even number
```

The Boolean expression under the *if* statement evaluated to a true hence the statement within the body of *if* statement has been executed.

If you need to get the number from the user, you can prompt them to enter the number using the *cin* function:

```cpp
#include <iostream>
```

```
using namespace std;
int main () {

int x;
    cout<<"Enter a Number: ";
    cin>>x;

            if (x % 2 == 0)
            {
                cout<<"X is an even number";
            }
            else
            {
                cout<<"X is an odd number";
            }
    return 0;
}
```

if...else if...else Statement

This statement should be used when there is a need to test multiple conditions. In this statement, you should begin by a single *if* statement, followed by any number of **else if** statement and lastly an *else* statement. The last statement, that is, **else** will be executed when none of the previous conditions have evaluated to a true. This syntax is given below:

```
if(expression 1) {
    // Executes when the expression 1 is true
} else if(expression 2) {
    // Executes when the expression 2 is true
} else if(expression 3) {
    // Executes when the expression 3 is true
} else {
```

```
    // executes when none of the above conditions
is true.
}
```

Let us create an example that demonstrates the above:

```cpp
#include <iostream>
using namespace std;

int main () {
    // local variable declaration:
    int x = 3;

    // check the boolean condition
    if( x == 1 ) {
        // if condition is true, print the
following
        cout << "Value of x is 1" << endl;
    } else if( x == 2 ) {
        // if else if condition is true
        cout << "Value of x is 2" << endl;
    } else if( x == 3 ) {
        // if else if condition is true
        cout << "Value of x is 3" << endl;
    } else {
        // if none of the conditions is true
        cout << "Value of x was not matched" <<
endl;
    }
    cout << "The exact value of x is : " << x <<
endl;

    return 0;
}
```

The code should return the following:

```
Value of x is 3
The exact value of x is : 3
```

We created the variable **x** and assigned it a value of **3**. Due to this, the following Boolean expression evaluated to a true:

```
} else if ( x == 3 ) {
```
The statement below was executed to give us the first line in the above output. We had also created a *cout* statement that is outside any of the conditions. This part must execute whether any condition is true or not. You can play around with the code by changing the value of variable x and see the kind of result that you get.

switch Statement

With the *switch* statement, we are able to test a variable against a set of values. Each value is referred to as a *case*, and the variable that is to be switched is checked against for every case. The following syntax explains this better:

```
switch(expression){
case value_1:
  //code for execution;
  break;
case value_2:
  //code for execution;
  break;
......

default:
  //code for execution if no case is matched;
  break;
}
```

Optionally, you can add a *default* case at the end of the switch to be evaluated if none of the cases is matched. Note that each case should be followed by a colon.

Let us create an example to demonstrate this:

```
#include <iostream>
using namespace std;
int main () {
        int num = 3;

        switch (num)
        {
            case 1: cout<<"The num is 1";
            break;

            case 2: cout<<"The num is 2";
            break;

            case 3: cout<<"The num is 3";
            break;

            case 4: cout<<"The num is 4";
            break;

            case 5: cout<<"The num is 5";
            break;

            default:
            cout<<"The num is not 1, 2, 3, 4 or
5";

            break;
        }
}
```

The code should print the following result:

```
The num is 3
```

We created a variable named *num* and assigned it a value of **3**. We have then created various cases running for values of *num* from 1 to **5**. The case of **3** was matched and the statement below it was executed giving us the above output. You can change the value of *num* to a value such as 10 and see the default part is executed.

If you are testing a string or a character, the values should be enclosed within quotes. For example:

```
        .
        .
        .
case 'A'
    :
        .
```

Nested if Statements

It is possible for us to nest *if...else* statements, which means that we can use an *if* or *else...if* statement inside another *if* or *else...if* statement. A **nested** *if* statement takes the syntax given below:

```
if(expression 1) {
    // To execute when expression 1 is true
    if(expression 2) {
        // To execute when expression 2 is true
    }
}
```

Consider the following example:

```
#include <iostream>
using namespace std;

int main () {
    // Declaration of a local variable:
    int x = 12;
    int y = 15;
```

```
    // checking the boolean condition
    if( x == 12 ) {
        // if above condition is true, then check
this condition
        if( y == 15 ) {
            // if condition is true, print the
following
            cout << "Value of x is 12 and y is 15"
<< endl;
        }
    }
    cout << "Exact value of x is : " << x << endl;
    cout << "Exact value of y is : " << y << endl;

    return 0;
}
```

The code returns the following result:

```
Value of x is 12 and y is 15
Exact value of x is : 12
Exact value of y is : 15
```

In our above example, we have declared two variables, **x,** and y, and initialized their values to **12** and **15** respectively. In the outer, *if* condition, we are checking whether the value of variable **x** is **12**. This is true, hence this condition evaluated to a true. Since the outer, *if* has evaluated to a *true,* the inner *if* was executed. In the inner *if,* we are checking whether the value of variable y is **15**, which is true. The value of the inner *if* has evaluated to a true. Due to this, the statement below it has been executed. This explains the source of the first line in the above output.

After the execution of the body of the two *if* statements, execution has jumped to the statements outside or immediately after the decision making statements. Note that these statements have to be executed, whether any of the *if* conditions are **true** or not.

If any of the *if* conditions evaluate to a false, then the statement below the inner *if* will not be executed. To see this, change the code to the following:

```cpp
#include <iostream>
using namespace std;

int main () {
    // Declaration of a local variable:
    int x = 12;
    int y = 15;

    // checking the boolean condition
    if( x == 10 ) {
        // if above condition is true, then check
this condition
        if( y == 15 ) {
            // if condition is true, print the
following
            cout << "Value of x is 12 and y is 15"
<< endl;
        }
    }
    cout << "Exact value of x is : " << x << endl;
    cout << "Exact value of y is : " << y << endl;

    return 0;
}
```

The value of variable **x** is **12**, but in our outer if, we are checking whether this value is **12**. This will evaluate to a false. The inner if will not be evaluated, but execution will jump to the statements outside the *ifs* to return the following output:

```
Exact value of x is : 12
Exact value of y is : 15
```

Nested switch Statement

This is a *switch* statement that is nested inside another *switch* statement. The case statements for both the outer and the inner switch may have common values, but these will not raise an error. Nested switch takes the following syntax:

```
switch(outer) {
    case 'A':
        cout << "This is an A of outer switch";
        switch(inner) {
            case 'A':
                cout "Thi is an A of inner switch";
                break;
            case 'B':
        }
        break;
    case 'B':
}
```

Let us create an example that demonstrates how to create such:

```
#include <iostream>
using namespace std;

int main () {
    // |Declaration of a local variable:
    int x = 12;
    int y = 15;

    switch(x) {
        case 12:
```

```cpp
            cout << "This is an outer switch" <<
endl;
        switch(y) {
            case 15:
                cout << "This is an inner switch"
<< endl;
            }
    }
    cout << "The value of x is : " << x << endl;
    cout << "The value of y is : " << y << endl;

    return 0;
}
```

The code will return the following output upon execution:

```
This is an outer switch
This is an inner switch
The value of x is : 12
The value of y is : 15
```

We have defined two variables, **x,** and **y**, and initialized their values to **12** and **15** respectively. We have tested these values using the *switch* statements. Since the switch statements were matched, they were both executed. The two statements outside the switch conditions have been executed. These must be executed whether the switch conditions are matched or not.

For the inner switch to be executed, the outer switch must be matched. This means that the inner switch relies on the outer switch. If the outer switch is not matched, the inner switch will not be evaluated. However, the outer switch will be evaluated whether the inner switch is matched or not. To test this changes the code to the following:

```cpp
#include <iostream>
using namespace std;
```

```cpp
int main () {
    // |Declaration of a local variable:
    int x = 12;
    int y = 15;

    switch(x) {
        case 10:
            cout << "This is an outer switch" <<
endl;
            switch(y) {
                case 15:
                    cout << "This is an inner switch"
<< endl;
            }
        }
    cout << "The value of x is : " << x << endl;
    cout << "The value of y is : " << y << endl;

    return 0;
}
```

In the above example, the value of **x** is **12**. The outer switch is matching this for 10, hence no matching will be made. Due to this, execution of the switch statements will halt and execution will jump to the statements outside these to return the following result:

```
The value of x is : 12
The value of y is : 15
```

Note that the inner switch was to be matched, that is, **15** to **15**, but because it relies on the outer switch, it was not evaluated. Let us change the code to the following:

```cpp
#include <iostream>
using namespace std;

int main () {
```

```cpp
// |Declaration of a local variable:
int x = 12;
int y = 15;

switch(x) {
    case 12:
        cout << "This is an outer switch" <<
endl;
        switch(y) {
            case 10:
                cout << "This is an inner switch"
<< endl;
        }
    }
    cout << "The value of x is : " << x << endl;
    cout << "The value of y is : " << y << endl;

    return 0;
}
```

The code will return the following:

```
This is an outer switch
The value of x is : 12
The value of y is : 15
```

The reason for the above output is that the outer switch is matched but the inner switch is not.

9 – C++
Functions

A function refers to a set of statements that perform related tasks. Every program in C++ has at least one function, which is the *main()* function and it is possible for more functions to be defined within the program.

A C++ program can be subdivided into a set of functions. The way you sub-divide the code lies up to you, but it should be done in such a way that every function performs a certain task.

When such code is grouped together and given a name, it becomes easy for you to reuse the code calling and calling it again through the function name. Again, the code will become optimized since there will be no need for you to write it again. Suppose your goal is to check three numbers, **150, 230** and **450** to tell whether they are even or not. Without the use of a function, you will have to write the logic for the even number each time. This will be a repetition of code. However, by use of a function, you can write the logic only once and keep on calling it.

Function Declaration

The work of a function declaration is to tell the C++ compiler about the name of the function, its return type and parameters. To define a function in C++, we use the following syntax:

```
returnType functionName(dataType parameter...)
{
//function body code
}
```

From the above syntax, you can tell that a function definition is made up of a header and function body.

A function can return any value. The ***returnType*** denotes the data type of the value returned by the function. However, there are functions that will perform their tasks without returning values. In such a case, the return type should be *void*.

The ***functionName*** is the name of the function. The ***functionName*** together with the parameter list form the function signature.

See a parameter as a ***placeholder***. When you invoke a function, you pass a value to the parameter. The value will be the actual parameter or argument. Note that each parameter is associated with a data type. Also, note that there are functions without parameters.

The function body should have statements defining what

the function should when invoked.

Here is an example of a simple function:

```cpp
#include <iostream>
using namespace std;
void myFunc() {
    static int x=0; //static variable
    int y=0; //local variable
    x++;
    y++;
    cout<<"x is: " << x<<" and y is: " <<y<<endl;
}
int main()
{
 myFunc();
 myFunc();
 myFunc();
}
```

The code should print the following output when executed:

```
x is: 1 and y is: 1
x is: 2 and y is: 1
x is: 3 and y is: 1
```

We have defined a function named *myFunc()*. The function takes no parameters and it is of void type, meaning that it returns nothing. Within the body of the function, we have defined one static variable x and one variable y. Their values have been initialized to 0. We have then called the increment operator on each of these two variables.

We have ended the body of the function *myFunc()*. Within the *main()* method, we have invoked the function *myFunc()* three times. Note that no parameter values have been passed during the invocation as our function takes no parameter. Since x is a static variable, the statement **x++** will increase the value of **x** by **1** per invocation, meaning we will get **1, 2** and **3**. This will be different for variable y as it has not been marked as static. It will return **1, 1** and **1** for the three invocations.

You now know why we have the above output.

Let us create an example of a function that takes in parameters:

```cpp
#include <iostream>
using namespace std;

// declare the function maxNum()
int maxNum(int x, int y);

int main () {
    // declare local variables
    int p;
    int q;
    int max;

    // call the function to get the maximum value.
    max = maxNum(5, 12);
    cout << "The maximum value is : " << max <<
endl;

    return 0;
}

// function returning the max between two numbers
int maxNum(int x, int y) {
    // local variable declaration
    int result;

    if (x > y)
        result = x;
    else
        result = y;
```

```
    return result;
}
```

The code should return the following as the result:

```
The maximum value is : 12
```

We began by declaring a function named *maxNum()* taking two integer arguments, **x,** and **y**. The function is of integer data type, meaning that its return value will be an integer. Within the *main()* method, we have invoked this function in the following line:

```
max = maxNum(5, 12);
```

What happens is that we have called the function and passed to it the value of the arguments. In the above line, the value of parameter x is **5** while that of parameter y is **12**. Order is very important. The result will be assigned to the variable named *max.*

Lastly, we have implemented the logic for our function. We want our function to return the larger of the two integers that we pass to it. The largest integer will be stored in the variable result. If the value of x is greater than that of y, then x will become the result. If y is greater than x, then y will become the result. That is what we have done in the function body.

In our above call, the function compared **5** and **12**. **12** was found to be the largest, hence, it became the result.

For any function that accepts arguments, it must declare

the variables that will be accepting the values of the arguments. The variables are referred to as the *formal parameters* of the function.

The formal parameters exhibit similar behavior as other local variables in the function and their creation happens after entry into the function and they are destroyed upon exit.

We pass the values of the arguments when calling or invoking the function as we did in our previous example. There are various ways through which we can pass the values of the arguments to the function. Let us discuss these:

Call by Value

This mechanism involves copying of the actual values of the parameters to the formal parameters of the function. Any changes made to the parameters inside the function will have no impact on the argument.

This is the default parameter passing mechanism used in C++. This means that the code in the function cannot change the arguments used for calling the function. Let us create a simple example to demonstrate this:

```cpp
#include <iostream>
using namespace std;
void substitute(int value);
int main()
{
int value = 2;
substitute(value);
cout << "The value is: " << value<< endl;
return 0;
}
```

```
void substitute(int value)
{
value = 10;
}
```

The code should return the following output:

```
The value is: 2
```

We have defined a function named ***substitute()*** that takes in one integer argument named ***value***. In the implementation of the function, we have set the value to 10. However, in the ***main()*** method, we changed this to **2**. That is why we have the above output. The pass by value was implemented in the following lines:

```
int value = 2;
substitute(value);
```

We initialized the value and passed the name to the function. That is how simple pass by value is.

Call by Pointer

This mechanism involves copying the address of the argument into the formal parameter. This address is then used to get the actual value of the argument inside the function. This means that if a change is done to the parameter, the argument will be affected.

To pass a value by pointer, the argument pointers should be passed to the functions similarly to any other value. This means that the function parameters should be defined as pointer types as demonstrated in the following snippet:

```cpp
// defining a function to swap values.
void interchange(int *a, int *b) {
    int temp;
    temp = *a; /* save value at address a */
    *a = *b; /* put b into a */
    *b = temp; /* put a into b */

    return;
}
```

Remember that a pointer * points to a memory location.

Let us create a complete code that demonstrates how this works:

```cpp
#include <iostream>
using namespace std;

// declare a function
void interchange(int *a, int *b);

int main () {
    // declare a local variable:
    int x = 5;
    int y = 12;

    cout << "Before the interachange, the value of
x is :" << x << endl;
    cout << "Before the interachange, the value of
y is :" << y << endl;

    /* call the function to interchange the
values.
        * &x indicates pointer to x, that is,
address of variable x and
        * &y indicates pointer to y, that is,
address of variable y.
    */
```

```
    interchange(&x, &y);

    cout << "After the interchange, the value of x
is :" << x << endl;
    cout << "After the interchange, the value of y
is :" << y << endl;

    return 0;
}
// defining a function to swap values.
void interchange(int *a, int *b) {
    int temp;
    temp = *a; /* save value at address a */
    *a = *b; /* put b into a */
    *b = temp; /* put a into b */

    return;
}
```

Through call by pointer, we were able to interchange the values stored in the two different addresses. The code returns the following upon execution:

```
Before the interachange, the value of x is :5
Before the interachange, the value of y is :12
After the interchange, the value of x is :12
After the interchange, the value of y is :5
```

Call by Reference

In call by reference, the reference of an argument is copied to the formal parameter. Inside the function, we use the reference to access the actual argument that has been used in the call. This is an indication that the changes that have been made to the parameter will affect the argument that is passed.

To pass a value by reference, the argument reference is passed to the functions similarly as any other value. This means that the function parameters have to be declared as reference types as demonstrated in the following example:

```cpp
// define a function to interchange values
void interchange(int &a, int &b) {
    int temp;
    temp = a; /* store the value at address a */
    a = b;    /* put b into a */
    b = temp; /* put a into b */

    return;
}
```

Again, we have the *interchange()* function that swaps the two values. Let us now see how we can call the function and pass the arguments by reference:

```cpp
#include <iostream>
using namespace std;

// declaration of a function:
void interchange(int &a, int &b);

int main () {
    // declaration of a local variable:
    int x = 5;
    int y = 12;

    cout << "Before the interchange, the value of
x is :" << x << endl;
    cout << "Before the interchange, the value of
y is :" << y << endl;

    /* call the interchange function to swap the
values through reference.*/
    interchange(x, y);
```

```
    cout << "After the interchange, the value of x
is :" << x << endl;
    cout << "After the interchange, the value of y
is :" << y << endl;

    return 0;
}
// defining a function to interchange values
void interchange(int &a, int &b) {
    int temp;
    temp = a; /* store the value at address a */
    a = b;    /* put b into a */
    b = temp; /* put a into b */

    return;
}
```

The code should return the following output upon execution:

```
Before the interchange, the value of x is :5
Before the interchange, the value of y is :12
After the interchange, the value of x is :12
After the interchange, the value of y is :5
```

That is how pass by reference works in C++.

Default Values for Parameters

After defining a function, it is possible for you to define the default values for the parameters. In such a case, the default value will be used as the value of the parameter when you call the function without passing the value of that parameter.

To assign default values for parameters, you use the

assignment operator during the function definition. When no
value is specified, that default value will be used as the value of
the parameter. However, if you pass a value for the parameter,
the default value will be ignored and the passed value will be
used instead.

The following example demonstrates this:

```cpp
#include <iostream>
using namespace std;

int product(int x, int y = 10) {
    int result;
    result = x * y;

    return (result);
}
int main () {
    // declare a local variable:
    int x = 12;
    int y = 5;
    int result;

    // call the product function to multiply the
values.
    result = product(x, y);
    cout << "The product is :" << result << endl;

    // call the product function with one argument
only
    result = product(x);
    cout << "The product is :" << result << endl;

    return 0;
}
```

The code should return the following result when
executed:

```
The product is :60
The product is :120
```

Consider the following statement extracted from the code:

```
int product(int x, int y = 10)
```

Above, we are defining a function named ***product()*** that takes two integer arguments, **x,** and **y**. If we don't pass a value for the parameter y during the function call, then the parameter **y** will be assigned a default value of **10**.

The function has been called for the first time in the following line:

```
result = product(x, y);
```

Above, the value of **x** is **12** while that of y is **5**. When the two are multiplied, we get a result of **60**, hence the source of the first line in the above output. The default value for parameter **y**, which is **10**, has been ignored because we have specified a value for the parameter during the call.

We have called the same function for the second time in the following line:

```
result = product(x);
```

Above, we have called the ***product()*** function but we have only passed one parameter to it, **x**. The value of **x** is still **12**. Since we have not specified the value for the parameter y, its default value of **10** specified during the declaration of the function will be used. The two are multiplied to return a result of **120**. The default value for the parameter has been used since we did not specify its value during the function call.

10-Arrays

An array is a data structure provided by C++. This does not mean that other programming languages don't have the array data structure.

The array data structure stores its elements sequentially and these elements must all belong to the same data type. This means that a single array cannot store numbers and strings together. The elements must belong to one data type.

With an array, you don't have to declare all the variables. What you do is that you declare a single array and give it a name, say *age*. You can then store the ages of different individuals into that array.

The elements of an array are stored at indexes. This means that we also access the elements using their indexes. The first element in the array is said to be at index **0** of the array while the last element is said to be at index **n-1**, where n is the total number of elements in the array. This means that in our *age* array, the elements will be stored as **age[0], age[1], age[2],** etc.

An array has a fixed size.

Array Declaration

Array declaration in C++ involves telling the C++ compiler the data type of the array elements, the array name and the number of elements to be stored in the array. An array is declared using the following syntax:

```
type array_Name [ arraySize ];
```

That is how we declare a one-dimensional array in C++. The *type* can be any valid C++ data type, the *array_Name* is the name you assign to the array while the *arraySize* is the number of elements you want to store in the array, and this must be an integer constant with a value greater than 0. Consider the following example:

```
int age[10];
```

In the above example, we declared an array named *age* to store **10** integer elements.

Array Initialization

Initialization here means adding or storing elements in the array. You can initialize the elements one by one or by using a single statement.

The following example demonstrates this:

```
int age[10] = {19, 21, 22, 20, 18, 22, 19, 17,
23, 28};
```

Note that in the [], we stated that our array will store **10** elements. This match the number of elements that we add between the **{ }**. That is why we have added exactly **10** elements within the **{ }**.

If you don't specify the size of the array, the array will only be large enough to hold the number of elements that have been initialized. For example:

```
int age[] = {19, 21, 22, 20, 18, 22, 19, 17, 23,
28};
```

In the above example, an array of size 10 will be created because we have added **10** elements into it.

To assign an element to the array, we use the index. For example:

```
age[4] = 23;
```

What the above statement does is that it adds the element **23** to index **4** of the array. This means that **23** will be the **5th** element in the array. Remember the array elements start at index **0**.

Accessing Array Values

To access an element of an array, we only have to index the array. We only have to place the index at which the element is located within square brackets after the array name. Consider the example given below:

```
int john = age[5]
```

What we are doing in the above statement is that we are accessing the value stored at index **5** or the **6th** element of the array named *age* and storing the value in a variable named *john*.

Let us create an example that helps us define a one-dimensional array in C++:

```
#include <iostream>
using namespace std;
int main()
{
int age[] = {19, 21, 22, 20, 18, 22, 19, 17, 23,
28};
        for (int x = 0; x < 10; x++)
        {
            cout<<age[x]<<"\n";
        }
}
```

We have our array *age* with 10 integer elements. We have then created a *for* loop to help us iterate through the elements of the array. The variable **x** has been used for this.

The code returns the following upon execution:

```
19
21
22
20
18
22
19
17
23
28
```

Multi-dimensional Arrays

In our previous examples, we have been creating one-dimensional arrays. To declare a multi-dimensional array in C++, we use the syntax given below:

```
type array_name[size1][size2]...[size_N];
```

Here is an example of how to declare a **3**-dimensional array:

```
int myArray[3][5][9];
```

A two-dimensional array forms the simplest form of a multi-dimensional array. See it as a list of one-dimensional arrays. A two-dimensional array of size **a**, **b** can be declared as follows:

```
type arrayName [ a ][ b ];
```

The *type* can be any C++ data type while the ***arrayName*** is any valid identifier in C++.

See a two-dimensional array as a table with rows and

columns. To initialize a two-dimensional array, we just specify the array row elements within curly braces { }. This is demonstrated below:

```
int a[2][3] = {
    {0, 1, 2},    /* elements for row at index 0
*/
    {4, 5, 6}  /* elements for row at index 1 */
};
```

In the above example, we have created a **2** by **3** array named *a*, meaning that we have **2** rows and **3** columns. We have also initialized the array values.

Notice that we have nested the curly braces to specify the elements for each row. However, these are optional. We could have done it as follows:

```
int a[2][3] = {0, 1, 2, 3, 4, 5, 6};
```

To access the elements of a two-dimensional array, we have to specify the row and column indexes where the element is stored in the array. Here is an example:

```
int value = a[1][2];
```

The above statement will access the element stored at row **1** and column **2** of the array named *a* and assign it to a variable named *value*.

In the following example, we create a two-dimensional array and use two loop variables to access the elements:

```
#include <iostream>
using namespace std;
```

```
int main () {
    // an array with 5 rows and 2 columns.
    int x[4][2] = { {0,0}, {1,4}, {2,6}, {3,8}};

    // output every element of the array
    for ( int a = 0; a < 4; a++ )
        for ( int b = 0; b < 2; b++ ) {

            cout << "x[" << a << "][" << b << "]: ";
            cout << x[a][b]<< endl;
        }

    return 0;
}
```

The code returns the following result upon execution:

```
x[0][0]: 0
x[0][1]: 0
x[1][0]: 1
x[1][1]: 4
x[2][0]: 2
x[2][1]: 6
x[3][0]: 3
x[3][1]: 8
```

We have created an array named **x** with **4** rows and **2** columns. We have then created two *for* loops. In the first *for* loop, we have defined the variable **a** *that* we have used to access the row indexes of the elements. In the second *for* loop, we have created the variable *b* that we have used to access the column indexes of the array elements.

Passing an Array to a Function

In C++, we are not allowed to pass the whole array as a function argument. However, the same functionality can be achieved when we pass a pointer to an array by specifying the name of the array without an index. This means that we only pass the name of the array. This is demonstrated by the following syntax:

```
function_name(array_name); //how pass an array to
a function
```

Let us now create an example that demonstrates this:

```cpp
#include <iostream>
using namespace std;
void displayElements(int arr[5]);
int main()
{
        int array1[5] = { 12, 21, 35, 42, 56 };
        int array2[5] = { 4, 16, 22, 36, 49 };
        displayElements(array1); //passing an
array to a function
        displayElements(array2);
}
void displayElements(int arr[5])
{
    cout << "The array elements are:"<< endl;
    for (int x = 0; x < 5; x++)
    {
                cout<<arr[x]<<"\n";
    }
}
```

The code should return the following result:

```
The array elements are:
12
21
35
42
56
The array elements are:
4
16
22
36
49
```

We have our two arrays namely **array1** and **array2**. Each array is storing **5** integer elements. We have then used the function named **displayElements()** to show the elements of the arrays. The iteration through the array elements was achieved using a **for** loop and creating the variable named **x**. Note that only the array names were passed to the function.

11-Strings

C++ provides us with two ways of representing strings. These include the following:

- **C-style** character string.
- Using the **string class**.

C-Style Character String

This was first introduced in C programming language and it was later adopted in C++. The string is a one-dimensional array of characters that is terminated by the null character '**\0**'. This means that a null-terminated string has characters making a string and then followed by a null.

Consider the example given below:

```
char salute[6] = {'H', 'e', 'l', 'l', 'o', '\0'};
```

In the above declaration, we have created a string that forms the **word Hello**. For the purpose of holding the null character at the end of our array, the character array is one more character longer than the number of characters that we have in the *string Hello.*

If we follow the rule for declaring arrays, the above can be declared as follows:

```
char salute[] = "Hello";
```

Note that you don't have to place the null character at the end of the string constant. The C++ compiler will automatically add the '**\0**' at the end of your string during the array initialization. Let us try to print our string:

```
#include <iostream>

using namespace std;

int main () {

    char salute[6] = {'H', 'e', 'l', 'l', 'o',
'\0'};

    cout << "The Hello message: ";
    cout << salute << endl;

    return 0;
}
```

The code will return the following output:

```
The Hello message: Hello
```

There are numerous functions that we can use to

manipulate null-terminated strings. They include the following:

- **strcpy(s1, s2);**

This method will copy a string s1 into the string s2.

- **strcat(s1, s2);**

The method will concatenate the string **s2** at the end of the string **s1**.

- **strlen(s1);**

This method will return the length of the string s1.

- **strcmp(s1, s2);**

Returns a 0 if strings s1 and s2 are similar. It will return less than **0** if **s1<s2** and greater than 0 if **s1>s2**.

- **strchr(s1, he);**

This will return a pointer to the first occurrence of character *he* in the string **s1**.

- **strstr(s1, s2);**

This will return the pointer to the first occurrence of string **s2** in string **s1**.

The following example demonstrates how to use some of the above functions:

```cpp
#include <iostream>
#include <cstring>
using namespace std;

int main () {

    char s1[10] = "Hello";
    char s2[10] = "Class";
    char s3[10];
    int  len ;

    // copy s1 into s3
    strcpy( s3, s1);
```

```
cout << "strcpy( s3, s1) : " << s3 << endl;

// concatenates s1 and s2
strcat( s1, s2);
cout << "strcat( s1, s2): " << s1 << endl;

// get total length of s1 after concatenation
len = strlen(s1);
cout << "strlen(s1) : " << len << endl;

return 0;
}
```

The code should return the following result:

```
strcpy( s3, s1) : Hello
strcat( s1, s2): HelloClass
strlen(s1) : 10
```

String Class

C++ provides us with a class named *string* that provides us with all the operations that we have discussed above and additional functionalities. The following example demonstrates this:

```
#include <iostream>
#include <string>

using namespace std;

int main () {

    string s1 = "Hello";
    string s2 = "Class";
    string s3;
    int  len ;
```

```cpp
// copy s1 into s3
s3 = s1;
cout << "s3 : " << s3 << endl;

// to concatenate s1 and s2
s3 = s1 + s2;
cout << "s1 + s2 : " << s3 << endl;

// total length of s3 after concatenation
len = s3.size();
cout << "s3.size() :  " << len << endl;

return 0;
}
```

The code will return the following upon execution:

```
s3 : Hello
s1 + s2 : HelloClass
s3.size() :  10
```

12-Pointers

Pointers make it easy for us to perform certain tasks in C++. However, there are tasks that we cannot perform with pointers.

A variable is simply a memory location and every memory location is associated with an address. To access this address, we can use the ampersand operator **(&)** as it denotes the address in memory. Let us create an example to demonstrate this:

```cpp
#include <iostream>

using namespace std;
int main () {
    int  x;
    char y[5];

    cout << "Address of variable x is: ";
    cout << &x << endl;

    cout << "Address of variable y is: ";
    cout << &y << endl;
```

```
    return 0;
}
```

The code will print the following:

```
Address of variable x is: 0x7ffdb3f0617c
Address of variable y is: 0x7ffdb3f06177
```

A pointer refers to a variable whose value is an address of another variable. Just like the way you do with constants and variables, you must declare a pointer before you can be able to use it. To declare a pointer, we use the following syntax:

```
type *variable-name;
```

The *type* in the above syntax is the base type of the pointer, and it must be a valid data type in C++. The *variable-name* denotes the name of the pointer variable. The symbol * is known as the *asterisk* and it is the same symbol you use as the multiplication operator. However, in this case, the asterisk helps you designate the variable as a pointer. The following are examples of valid pointer declarations in C++:

```
int    *ix;    // pointer to integer
double *dx;    // pointer to double
float  *fx;    // pointer to a float
char   *ch     // pointer to a character
```

The following example demonstrates how to declare and

use a pointer in C++:

```
#include <iostream>
using namespace std;
int main () {
    int   x = 5;    // variable declaration.
    int  *ip;          // a pointer variable

    ip = &x;          // to store the address of x in
the pointer variable

    cout << "The value of variable x is: ";
    cout << x << endl;

    // return the address of ip pointer variable
    cout << "Address stored in the ip variable is:
";
    cout << ip << endl;

    cout << "Value of *ip variable: ";
    cout << *ip << endl;

    return 0;
}
```

The code will return the following output:

```
The value of variable x is: 5
Address stored in the ip variable is: 0x7ffd7ee79e64
Value of *ip variable: 5
```

13-Classes and Objects

The main difference between C and C++ programming languages is that the latter introduced the features of object-oriented programming. Classes and objects are examples of such features.

A class is simply a blueprint for an object. It acts as a template from which we create objects. The class combines data and methods for manipulating that data into one package. The data and functions contained within a class are referred to as the *class members*.

Class Definition

A class is a blueprint for a data type. Defining a class means giving the class a name, which will, in turn, determine the kind of data that an object of that class will have and the kind of operations that it will allow. A class definition doesn't define the data for the class.

To define a C++ class, we use the ***class*** keyword followed by the name of the class and then the body of the class. The beginning of the class body is marked by an opening curly brace { while the end of the class body is marked by a closing curly brace }. The class members are then defined within the body, that is, within the { }. Here is an example:

```
class Rectangle {
   public:
       double length;    // Length of the rectangle
       double breadth;   // Breadth of the
rectangle
};
```

In the above example, we have defined a class named ***Rectangle***. See the ***Rectangle*** as a data type. The class has two members/attributes, that is, length and breadth. Notice the use of the ***public*** keyword. It determines the access attributes of these two members. It means that they are accessible publicly, that is, from within the entire package. There are also other access modifiers like ***private*** and ***protected***.

Object Definition

We stated that a class is a blueprint for an object, meaning that we create objects from classes. The objects of a class are defined in the same way that we declare variables of different data types.

In our case, we have a class or a blueprint called Rectangle. We have two rectangles with different measurements, Rectangle1 and Rectangle 2. We can create them as follows:

```
Rectangle Rectangle1;          // Declare
Rectangle 1 of type Rectangle
Rectangle Rectangle2;          // Declare
Rectangle2 of type Rectangle
```

The objects **Rectangle1** and **Rectangle2** are of type Rectangle. It is of the same way we declare variables **x** and **y** of type int. Each of these two objects will have their own set of members.

Accessing Data Members

Our class has two data members, length and breadth and these have been declared as public. Because of this, we can access them by use of the direct member access operator (**.**). The following example will make it easy for you to understand this:

```cpp
#include <iostream>

using namespace std;

class Rectangle {
   public:
        double length;    // Length of the rectangle
        double breadth;   // Breadth of the
rectangle
};
```

```cpp
int main() {
    Rectangle Rectangle1;        // Declare
Rectangle 1 of type Rectangle
    Rectangle Rectangle2;        // Declare
Rectangle2 of type Rectangle

    double area = 0.0;        // to store the area of
the rectangle

    // rectangle 1 specification
    Rectangle1.length = 6.0;
    Rectangle1.breadth = 5.0;

    // rectangle 2 specification
    Rectangle2.length = 12.0;
    Rectangle2.breadth = 10.0;

    // area of rectangle 1
    area = Rectangle1.length * Rectangle1.breadth;
    cout << "Area of Rectangle1 : " << area
<<endl;

    // area of rectangle 2
    area = Rectangle2.length * Rectangle2.breadth;
    cout << "Area of Rectangle2 : " << area
<<endl;
    return 0;
}
```

The code should give you the following result:

```
Area of Rectangle1 : 30
Area of Rectangle2 : 120
```

Consider the following statements extracted from the code:

```cpp
Rectangle1.length = 6.0;
Rectangle1.breadth = 5.0;
```

We are using the object named Rectangle1 to access the

members of the Rectangle class, that is, length and breadth.
This is because **Rectangle1** is an object of type *Rectangle*,
hence, it has the properties of the **Rectangle** class. This means
that **Rectangle1** has a length, which we have initialized to **6.0**
and a breadth which we have initialized to **5.0**.

Here is another section extracted from the code:

```
Rectangle2.length = 12.0;
Rectangle2.breadth = 10.0;
```

Rectangle2 is an object of type **Rectangle,** hence, it has
both a length and a breadth. These have been initialized to **12.0**
and 10.0 respectively.

Here is another statement extracted from the code:

```
area = Rectangle1.length * Rectangle1.breadth;
```

We are multiplying the value of the length and width
assigned to the object named **Rectangle1** and storing the result
to the variable named *area*. This will be the area of the object
Rectangle1. This will be **6.0 * 5.0** to give **30.0**.

Here is another statement extracted from the code:

```
area = Rectangle2.length * Rectangle2.breadth;
```

We are multiplying the value of the length and width
assigned to the object named **Rectangle2** and storing the result
to the variable named *area*. This will be the area of the object
Rectangle2. This will be **12.0 * 10.0** to give **120.0.**

We were able to access the members of the class Rectangle
from our two objects, **Rectangle1** and **Rectangle2**.

Daniel Bell

Class Member functions

In our previous example, we had two members of the class Rectangle, length, and breadth. We can have a function defined within a class, and this can be referred to a class member function. Such a function can be accessed from objects of that class and it can access all the members of that class.

The length and breadth members were accessed directly. However, it is possible for us to access them using a member function. This is what we want to demonstrate. Consider the following code:

```
class Rectangle {
    public:
        double length;    // Length of the rectangle
        double breadth;   // Breadth of the
rectangle
        double getArea(void);// Returns rectangle
area

};
```

Above, we have our usual members of the class, length, and breadth. In addition to that, we have defined a member function named **getArea()**.

There are two ways through which we can define the member functions of a class. First, we can define them directly within the class. This means that the function is defined inline as shown below:

```
class Rectangle {
    public:
        double length;    // Length of the rectangle
        double breadth;   // Breadth of the
rectangle
```

```
double getArea(void) {
        return length * breadth;
    }
};
```

Note that the function ***getArea()*** in the above example has been defined within the body of the class Rectangle. The body of the class is marked by **{** and **};**. The function ***getArea()*** also has a body marked by **{** and **}**. Inside the function body, we have defined what the function will do, that is, multiplying the value of length with the value of breadth.

The second way of defining functions involves doing the definition outside the class by use of the ***scope resolution operator*** (::). The following example demonstrates this:

```
double Rectangle::getArea(void) {
    return length * breadth;
}
```

The important issue in the above example is that you should add the class name before the scope resolution operator.

After defining the function, we can access it by use of the dot operator (.). We only have to add the name of the object accessing the class member function before the dot operator.

Here is an example:

```
Rectangle Rectangle1;           // Creating an
object
Rectangle1.getArea();    // Call a member function
for the object
```

We have created an object named Rectangle1 of type

Rectangle. We have then used this object to access the member function of the Rectangle class.

Consider the following example:

```cpp
#include <iostream>

using namespace std;

class Rectangle {
   public:
      double length;    // Length of the rectangle
      double breadth;   // Breadth of the
rectangle

      //declaring the member functions
      double getArea(void);
      void setLength( double len );
      void setBreadth( double bre );

};


// Defintions of member functions
double Rectangle::getArea(void) {
   return length * breadth;
}

void Rectangle::setLength( double len ) {
   length = len;
}
void Rectangle::setBreadth( double bre ) {
   breadth = bre;
}


int main() {
   Rectangle Rectangle1;        // Declare
Rectangle 1 of type Rectangle
   Rectangle Rectangle2;        // Declare
Rectangle2 of type Rectangle
```

```
    double area = 0.0;       // to store the area of
the rectangle


    Rectangle1.setLength(6.0);
    Rectangle1.setBreadth(5.0);

    // box 2 specification
    Rectangle2.setLength(12.0);
    Rectangle2.setBreadth(10.0);



    // area of rectangle 1
    area = Rectangle1.getArea();
    cout << "Area of Rectangle1 : " << area
<<endl;

    // area of rectangle 2
    area = Rectangle2.getArea();
    cout << "Area of Rectangle2 : " << area
<<endl;
    return 0;
}
```

The code will return the following result:

```
Area of Rectangle1 : 30
Area of Rectangle2 : 120
```

We have defined three member functions for the class, namely *getArea(), setLength()* and *setBreadth()*. The declaration of these methods was done within the class body. However, their definitions were done outside the class body. We were then able to access these function from the objects of the class.

Access Modifiers

Data hiding is a great feature in any object-oriented programming language including C++. With information hiding, the functions of a program are prevented from having direct access to the internal representation of a class. The access can be restricted by labelling the class members as either public, private or protected. These keywords are known as *access specifiers.*

It is possible for us to have multiple class sections labeled as private, public or protected. The default access specifier for classes and its members is *private.* The following syntax specifies how these access specifiers can be used:

```
class ClassName {
    public:
        // public members should go here
        protected:

    // protected members should go here
    private:
    // private members should go here

};
```

Let discuss these:

Public Access Specifier

Any class member set as the *public* can be accessed from anywhere outside a class but within the program. The values of public variables can be set and accessed without using any member function. The following example demonstrates this:

```cpp
#include <iostream>

using namespace std;

class Person {
   public:
      double height;
      void setHeight( double heig );
      double getHeight( void );
};

// Definitions of member functions
double Person::getHeight(void) {
   return height ;
}

void Person::setHeight( double heig) {
   height = heig;
}

// Main function
int main() {
   Person person;

   // set person height
   person.setHeight(8.0);
   cout << "Height of person : " <<
person.getHeight() <<endl;

   // set person height without a member function
   person.height = 9.0; // since height is public
   cout << "Height of person : " << person.height
<<endl;

   return 0;
}
```

The code will return the following result:

```
Height of person : 8
Height of person : 9
```

We have successfully accessed all the members declared as public.

Private Access Specifier

A member function or variable declared as private cannot be accessed or viewed from outside a class. It's only the class and the friend functions that can access the private members.

The default setting is that all members are private, meaning that if a member is not labeled otherwise, it will become private. Here is an example:

```
class Rectangle {
    double breadth;

    public:
        double length;
        void setBreadth( double brea );
        double getBreadth( void );
};
```

In the above example, the member **breadth** has been declared without specifying its access type. Due to this, it will become a private member by default. The rest have been marked as public.

In most cases, data members are defined as private while functions are defined as public so that they can be called from outside the class. The following example demonstrates this:

```
#include <iostream>

using namespace std;

class Rectangle {
```

```cpp
public:
    double length;
    void setBreadth( double brea );
    double getBreadth( void );

private:
    double breadth;
};

// Definition of member functions
double Rectangle::getBreadth(void) {
    return breadth ;
}

void Rectangle::setBreadth( double brea ) {
    breadth = brea;
}

// Main function
int main() {
    Rectangle rectangle;

    // set rectangle length without a member
function
    rectangle.length = 12.0; // since length is
public
    cout << "Length of rectangle : " <<
rectangle.length <<endl;

    // set rectangle breadth without a member
function
    // rectangle.breadth = 10.0; // Error: because
breadth is private
    rectangle.setBreadth(10.0);  // Use a member
function to set it.
    cout << "Breadth of rectangle : " <<
rectangle.getBreadth() <<endl;

    return 0;
}
```

The code will return the following result after execution:

```
Length of rectangle : 12
Breadth of rectangle : 10
```

See that we have to use a member function to access a private member, which was not the case with public members.

Protected Access Specifier

A protected member function or variable is very similar to a private member function or variable but it comes with an additional benefit in that it can be accessed in the child classes which are known as *derived classes*.

Consider the example given below:

```cpp
#include <iostream>
using namespace std;

class Rectangle {
   protected:
      double breadth;
};

class SmallRectangle:Rectangle { //
SmallRectangle is a derived class.
   public:
      void setSmallBreadth( double brea );
      double getSmallBreadth( void );
};

// Member functions of the child class
double SmallRectangle::getSmallBreadth(void) {
   return breadth ;
}
```

```
void SmallRectangle::setSmallBreadth( double brea
) {
   breadth = brea;
}

// Main function
int main() {
   SmallRectangle rectangle;

   // set rectangle breadth using a member
function
   rectangle.setSmallBreadth(10.0);
   cout << "Breadth of rectangle : "<<
rectangle.getSmallBreadth() << endl;

   return 0;
}
```

When executed, the code will return the following:

```
Breadth of rectangle : 10
```

In the above example, we declared a class named Rectangle and within this class, we declared a protected member named **breadth**.

Consider the following line extracted from the code:

```
class SmallRectangle:Rectangle
```

What we are doing is that we are creating a child/derived class known SmallRectangle from the class Rectangle. This process is known as *inheritance*. We will discuss it later. The child class was then able to access the member from the base class that has been marked as protected, which the **breadth**.

Class Constructor

A class constructor refers to a special member function that is executed anytime a new object of the class is created.

A constructor should be given the same name as the class and it must not have a return type, even void. Constructors become very useful when we need to set the initial values of some class member variables.

Consider the example given below:

```cpp
using namespace std;

class Person {
    public:
        void setHeight( double heig );
        double getHeight( void );
        Person();  // This is the constructor
    private:
        double height;
};

// Definitions of member functions and the
// constructor
Person::Person(void) {
    cout << "Object is being created" << endl;
}
void Person::setHeight( double heig ) {
    height = heig;
}
double Person::getHeight( void ) {
    return height;
}

// Main function
int main() {
    Person person;

    // set person height
    person.setHeight(9.0);
```

```
    cout << "Height of person : " <<
person.getHeight() <<endl;

    return 0;
}
```

The code should return the following:

```
Object is being created
Height of person : 9
```

We have declared the class named Person. The constructor has been declared and given the same name as the class. This has been done in the following line of the code:

```
Person();
```

Parameterized Constructor

A default constructor takes no parameters, but it is possible for us to create a constructor that takes in parameters. This way, an initial value can be assigned to an object during the time of its creation. Here is an example:

```
class Person {
    public:
        void setHeight( double heig );
        double getHeight( void );
        Person(double heig);  // This is the
constructor
    private:
        double height;
};

// Definitions of member functions and the
constructor
```

```cpp
Person::Person(double heig) {
    cout << "Object is being created" << endl;
}
void Person::setHeight( double heig ) {
    height = heig;
}
double Person::getHeight( void ) {
    return height;
}

// Main function
int main() {
    Person person(8.0);
        cout << "Height of person : " <<
person.getHeight() <<endl;


    // set person height
    person.setHeight(9.0);
    cout << "Height of person : " <<
person.getHeight() <<endl;

    return 0;
}
```

Class Destructor

A destructor refers to a special member function of a class executed anytime an object of the class goes out of scope or anytime a delete operation is done on a pointer to the class object.

A destructor takes the same name as a class but it must be preceded with a tilde (~). A destructor doesn't take parameters and it does not return values. Destructors are good when you need to release resources like the closing of a file before you can leave a program. Here is an example demonstrating the use of a destructor:

```cpp
#include <iostream>

#include <iostream>

using namespace std;
#include <iostream>

using namespace std;
class Person {
   public:
      void setHeight( double heig );
      double getHeight( void );
      Person();   // Declaration of the
constructor
      ~Person();   // Declaration of the
destructor

   private:
      double height;
};

// Definitions of member functions and the
constructor
Person::Person (void) {
   cout << "Object is being created" << endl;
}
Person::~Person(void) {
   cout << "Object is being deleted" << endl;
}
void Person::setHeight( double heig ) {
   height = heig;
}
double Person::getHeight( void ) {
   return height;
}

// Main function
int main() {
   Person person;

   // set person height
```

```
    person.setHeight(9.0);
    cout << "Height of person : " <<
person.getHeight() <<endl;

    return 0;
}
```

The code should return the following result:

```
Object is being created
Height of person : 9
Object is being deleted
```

14-Inheritance

Inheritance is a very important concept of object-oriented programming. With inheritance, we are able to define one class in terms of another class.

During the creation of a new class, instead of defining new data members and functions for the class, we can state that the new classes will inherit these from an already existing class.

Inheritance is simply an implementation of the is a relationship. For example, Harrier IS-A car, cow IS-A mammal, etc.

Base and Derives Classes

It is possible for a class to inherit data and function members from multiple classes, meaning that it can inherit from multiple base classes. To define a base class, we have to use a class derivation list to state the base classes. A class derivation list will name one or more class and it takes the following form:

```
class derived-class: access-specifier base-class
```

The access-specifier in the above class can be private, public or protected while the base-class is the name of the class. If you don't specify the access specifier, then it will become private by default.

Consider the example given below:

```cpp
#include <iostream>

using namespace std;

// The base class
class Figure {
   public:
       void setBreadth(int b) {
          breadth = b;
       }
       void setLength(int l) {
          length = l;
       }

   protected:
       int breadth;
       int length;
};

// Derived class
class Rectangle: public Figure {
   public:
       int getArea() {
          return (breadth * length);
       }
};

int main(void) {
   Rectangle Rect;
```

```
Rect.setBreadth(7);
Rect.setLength(8);

// Return area of the rectangle.
cout << "Rectangle area is: " <<
Rect.getArea() << endl;

    return 0;
}
```

The code should return the following output:

```
Rectangle area is: 56
```

In the above example, we have Figured as the base class and Rectangle as the derived class. Rect is an object of Rectangle class and it was able to access the member functions defined in the base class. Note that these functions had been marked as public using the ***public*** access specifier. We also accessed the two data members, breadth and length defined in the base class. These had been marked as protected using the ***protected*** access specifier.

Multiple Inheritance

Multiple inheritance is said to have occurred when a C++ class inherits from more than one base classes. This is done using the following syntax:

```
class derived-class: access-specifier base_A,
access-specifier base_B...
```

The derived-class is the name to be given to the derived

class, **base_A** is the name of the first base class, **base_B** the name of the second base class.... and **access_specifier** is the level of access of a class, which can be private, public or protected.

Here is an example:

```cpp
#include <iostream>

using namespace std;

// Base class Shape
class Figure {
    public:
    void setBreadth(int b) {
        breadth = b;
    }
    void setLength(int l) {
        length = l;
    }

    protected:
        int breadth;
        int length;
};


// Base class ColorCost
class ColorCost {
    public:
        int getCost(int area) {
            return area * 50;
        }
};

// Derived class
class Rectangle: public Figure, public ColorCost
{
    public:
        int getArea() {
            return (breadth * length);
```

```cpp
        }
};

int main(void) {
    Rectangle Rect;
    int area;

        Rect.setBreadth(7);
    Rect.setLength(8);

        area = Rect.getArea();


    // Return area of the rectangle.
    cout << "Rectangle area is: " <<
Rect.getArea() << endl;

    // Print the total cost of painting
    cout << "Total painting cost is: $" <<
Rect.getCost(area) << endl;

    return 0;
}
```

The code will return the following output:

```
Rectangle area is: 56
Total painting cost is: $2800
```

15-Overloading

In C++, it is possible for us to specify more than one definition for a function or operator within the same scope. These are processes known as *function overloading* and *operator overloading* respectively.

An overloaded declaration is done within the same scope as the previous declaration but both definitions have different arguments and a different implementation/definition.

After calling an overloaded function or operator, the compiler will determine the most appropriate definition to use by comparing the types of arguments that you have used to call the function or operator with the types of parameters that have been specified in the definition. The process of determining the most appropriate definition to use is referred to as *overload resolution.*

Function Overloading

You can have different functions of one function within one scope. To create the variation between function definitions, you can use different types or number of parameters for the different functions. Here is an example:

```cpp
#include <iostream>
using namespace std;
class MyClass {
    public:
static int add(int x,int y){
        return x + y;
    }
static int add(int x, int y, int z)
    {
        return x + y + z;
    }
};
int main(void) {
    MyClass C;  //       class object declaration.
    cout<<C.add(1, 2)<<endl;
    cout<<C.add(1, 2, 3);
    return 0;
}
```

In the above class we have two definitions of the function *add()* within the same scope. In the first definition, the function takes two integer arguments, **x** and **y**. In the second definition, the function takes three integer arguments, **x, y** and **z.**

When calling the functions, the number of arguments we passed determined the definition to be invoked. For the two arguments, the first definition has been invoked. For three arguments, the second definition has been invoked.

The code should return the following output:

Operators Overloading

C++ allows you to re-define or overload the majority of its in-built operators. This means that programmers can use operators with user-defined types.

Overloaded operators are simple functions with special names, that is, the ***operator*** keyword and then then symbol of the operator that is under the definition. Just like a function definition, an overloaded operator will have a return type and a list of parameters. The definition of an overloaded operator is demonstrated below:

```
Rectangle operator+(const Rectangle&);
```

In the above example, we have defined the addition operator that we can use to add two rectangle objects and it returns the final Figure object. We can define most overloaded operators as ordinary non-member functions or as class member functions. If the above function was to be defined as a non-member function of a class, then we would have passed the two arguments for every operand as shown below:

```
Rectangle operator+(const Rectangle&, const
Rectangle&);
```

In the example given below, we are demonstrating the

process of operator overloading by the use of a member function. We will pass an object as an argument and the properties of the object will be accessed using the object, and the object that will call the operator will be accessible by use of the *this* operator as demonstrated below:

```cpp
#include <iostream>
using namespace std;

class Rectangle {
    public:
        double getArea(void) {
            return length * breadth;
        }
        void setLength( double len ) {
            length = len;
        }
        void setBreadth( double bre ) {
            breadth = bre;
        }

        // Overload the + operator to add two
Rectangle objects.
        Rectangle operator+(const Rectangle& r) {
            Rectangle rect;
            rect.length = this->length + r.length;
            rect.breadth = this->breadth +
r.breadth;
            return rect;
        }

    private:
        double length;      // Length of a
rectangle
        double breadth;      // Breadth of a
rectangle
};

// Main function
int main() {
```

```
    Rectangle Rectangle1;      // Declare Rectangle1
of type Rectangle
    Rectangle Rectangle2;      // Declare Rectangle2
of type Rectangle
    Rectangle Rectangle3;      // Declare Rectangle3
of type Rectangle
    double area = 0.0;         // Store the area of a
Rectangle here

    // Rectangle 1 specification
    Rectangle1.setLength(6.0);
    Rectangle1.setBreadth(7.0);

    // Rectangle 2 specification
    Rectangle2.setLength(12.0);
    Rectangle2.setBreadth(13.0);

    // area of Rectangle 1
    area = Rectangle1.getArea();
    cout << "Area of Rectangle1 : " << area
<<endl;

    // area of Rectangle 2
    area = Rectangle2.getArea();
    cout << "Area of Rectangle2 : " << area
<<endl;

    // Adding two objects:
    Rectangle3 = Rectangle1 + Rectangle2;

    // area of rectangle 3
    area = Rectangle3.getArea();
    cout << "Area of Rectangle3 : " << area
<<endl;

    return 0;
}
```

When executed, the code will return the following:

```
Area of Rectangle1 : 42
Area of Rectangle2 : 156
Area of Rectangle3 : 360
```

Consider the following section extracted from the above code:

```
Rectangle operator+(const Rectangle& r) {
        Rectangle rect;
        rect.length = this->length + r.length;
        rect.breadth = this->breadth +
r.breadth;
        return rect;
    }
```

This is where the mechanism of operator overloading has been implemented. We have overloaded the **+** operator so that it adds the measurements of two rectangle objects. Here is another line extracted from the code:

```
Rectangle3 = Rectangle1 + Rectangle2;
```

In the above line, **Rectangle1** will be added to **Rectangle2**. This means that the length of **Rectangle1** will be added to the length of **Rectangle2** to get the length of **Rectangle3** while the breadth of **Rectangle1** will be added to the breadth of **Rectangle2** to get the breadth of **Rectangle3**. These two will then be multiplied to give the area of **Rectangle3**.

The meaning of + operator has been overloaded!

16-
Polymorphism

Polymorphism means to exist in many forms. In programing, polymorphism occurs when we have many classes that are related to each other through inheritance.

In C++, polymorphism means that a call to a function will lead to the execution of a different function depending on the type of object that has invoked the function. Consider the example given below in which we have a base class derived or inherited by two other classes:

```cpp
#include <iostream>
using namespace std;

class Figure {
    protected:
        int breadth, length;

    public:
```

```cpp
        Figure( int x = 0, int y = 0){
            breadth = x;
            length = y;
        }
        int area() {
            cout << "Area of parent class is :"
<<endl;
            return 0;
        }
};
class Rectangle: public Figure {
    public:
        Rectangle( int x = 0, int y = 0):Figure(x,
y) { }

        int area () {
            cout << "Area of Rectangle class is :"
<<endl;
            return (breadth * length);
        }
};

class Square: public Figure {
    public:
        Square( int x = 0, int y = 0):Figure(x, y)
{ }

        int area () {
            cout << "Area of Square class is :"
<<endl;
            return (breadth * length);
        }
};

// Main function
int main() {
    Figure *figure;
    Rectangle rec(10,7);
    Square  sq(5,5);

    // store address of Rectangle
    figure = &rec;
```

```
// call rectangle area.
figure->area();

// store the address of Square
figure = &sq;

// call aquare area.
figure->area();

return 0;
}
```

The code will return the following output:

```
Area of parent class is :
Area of parent class is :
```

The output is incorrect. The reason for this is that the call of *area()* function has been set only once by the compiler as the version that has been defined in the base class. |This is referred to as *static resolution* or *static linkage* of the function call. The function call is fixed before the execution of the program. Sometimes, this is referred to as *early binding* since our area has been set during the compilation of the program.

Let us make a modification to the code so that the *area()* function is declared within the Figure class. However, we will declare it with the *virtual* keyword as shown below:

```
class Figure {
   protected:
      int breadth, length;

   public:
      Figure( int x = 0, int y = 0){
         breadth = x;
         length = y;
      }
```

```
        virtual int area() {
            cout << "Area of parent class is :"
<<endl;
            return 0;
        }
};
```

This means you should now have the following code:

```
#include <iostream>
using namespace std;

class Figure {
    protected:
        int breadth, length;

    public:
        Figure( int x = 0, int y = 0){
            breadth = x;
            length = y;
        }
        virtual int area() {
            cout << "Area of parent class is :"
<<endl;
            return 0;
        }
};
class Rectangle: public Figure {
    public:
        Rectangle( int x = 0, int y = 0):Figure(x,
y) { }

        int area () {
            cout << "Area of Rectangle class is :"
<<endl;
            return (breadth * length);
        }
};

class Square: public Figure {
    public:
```

```
        Square( int x = 0, int y = 0):Figure(x, y)
  { }

        int area () {
            cout << "Area of Square class is :"
<<endl;
            return (breadth * length);
        }
};

// Main function
int main() {
    Figure *figure;
    Rectangle rec(10,7);
    Square  sq(5,5);
    // store address of Rectangle
    figure = &rec;

    // call rectangle area.
    figure->area();

    // store the address of Square
    figure = &sq;

    // call aquare area.
    figure->area();

    return 0;
}
```

The code should now return the following result:

```
Area of Rectangle class is :
Area of Square class is :
```

The compiler has considered the elements of the pointer rather than its type. The objects of *rec* and *sq* classes have been stored in the *figure, their respective definition of the *area()* function have been called.

This shows that each of the derived classes has a different implementation of the function named *area()*. This is known as *polymorphism*. You have more than one class with the same function name and the same parameters, but the implementation is different.

Notice that we used the *virtual* keyword to make the function virtual. When a virtual function is defined in the base class, and another version in the derived class, this will act as a signal to the compiler that a static linkage to the function is not needed. We only need a selection of the function to be called at any point in the program based on the type of object for which the function is being called. This operation is known as *late binding* or *dynamic linkage*.

Sometimes, you may be in need of including a virtual function in the base class for it to be redefined in a derived class to suit the class objects, but you have no meaningful definition to give to the function in the base class.

In such a case, our virtual function *area()* in the base class can be changed to the following:

```
class Figure {
    protected:
        int breadth, length;

    public:
        Figure( int x = 0, int y = 0){
            breadth = x;
            length = y;
        }

        virtual int area() = 0;
};
```

Daniel Bell

Notice the use of the = **0**; in the function. This tells the C++ compiler that the function doesn't have a body. Such a function is known as a ***pure virtual function***.

17-Data Abstraction

Data abstraction is another important concept provided in object-oriented programming languages. It occurs when the user is provided with only what is necessary to the outside world while hiding the implementation details from the user.

With data abstraction, we are able to separate the user interface from the implementation. Consider the example of a car. When you are driving and you press the accelerator, you see the car increase its speed when you press the brakes, you see the car stop. However, you don't know the mechanical movements that happen internally to make the car accelerate or stop. You have only been presented with what is necessary for you.

Due to this, we can say that a car separates its internal implementation details from the external interface and you can play around with the brake, the accelerator steering wheel, etc.

without knowing what happens internally.

In C++, abstraction is provided by classes. They provide enough public methods to the outside world to play around with the functionality of an object and to modify the object data without knowing how the class has been implemented internally. You can call a method such as a *sort* and it will sort your values without you knowing the type of algorithm that the algorithm uses to sort the values.

Classes help us to define abstract data types (ADTs). Consider the following code:

```cpp
#include <iostream>
using namespace std;

int main() {
    cout << "Hello there!" <<endl;
    return 0;
}
```

Above, we have used the **cout** object defined in the **ostream** class to stream data to the standard output. you are not required to know how the cout object works to display text on your screen.

Anytime that you create a class in C++ with private and public members, you implement abstraction. Here is an example:

```cpp
#include <iostream>
using namespace std;

class Sum {
    public:
        // The constructor
        Sum(int x = 0) {
```

```cpp
            total = x;
        }

        // interface to the external world
        void sumNum(int number) {
            total += number;
        }

        // interface to ethe xternal world
        int getTotal() {
            return total;
        };

    private:
        // data hideen from the outside world
        int total;
};

int main() {
    Sum s;

    s.sumNum(5);
    s.sumNum(12);
    s.sumNum(3);

    cout << "The sum is " << s.getTotal() <<endl;
    return 0;
}
```

The code will return the following result:

The sum is 20

We have created a class whose work is to add three numbers and return their sum. We have two members that have been made public, *sumNum()* and *getTotal()*. a user only needs to know them and be able to use the class. We have also created a hidden member named *total*. The user does not need to know more about this member but it is required for the class to function in the way that it is intended to function.

Through abstraction, we are able to separate the code into two, the interface and the implementation. This means that when you are implementing your C++ app, you have to keep the interface independent of the implementation. This will mean that if you make a change to the implementation, the interface will still remain intact, that would mean that programs using the interfaces will not be affected and they will only need a recompilation so as to be able to use the latest implementation.

Conclusion

This marks the end of this guide. C++ is a computer programming language. It was developed to make number improvements to the then C programming language. C is a structured programming language whereas C++ is an object-oriented programming language. This means that C introduced object-oriented programming features to the C programming language. Object oriented programming involves the treatment of items as objects. This is what C++ does. It is a case sensitive programming language, meaning that it differentiates between uppercase from lowercase letters. You have to be keen when naming and referring/calling objects in C++ so that you may call them using the right case according to their definition.

To program in C++, you only a text editor and the C++ compiler. The text editor will provide you with an environment where you will write your C++ programs. It is recommended that you give your C++ source files a .cpp extension to mark them C++ files. It is the default extension used by the C++ compiler. The purpose of the C++ compiler is to process your C++ source file to give you the result. There are many ways through which you can get this into your computer depending on the type of operating system you are using on your computer. For the case of the text editor, you can for the basic ones like Notepad on Windows and vim for Windows and Linux/Unix. Once you have assembled these, you can write, compile and execute C++ programs on your computer.

ABOUT THE AUTHOR

Daniel Bell was born in the Bronx, New York. When he was nine, he moved with his father Guy Bell to Nice in France. He received his Ph.D. degree in computer science from the University of Nice (France) in 2012. Daniel is conducting research in data management, with an emphasis on topics related to Big Data and data sharing, such as probabilistic data, data pricing, parallel data processing, data security. He spends his free time in the writing of books on computer programming and data science, to help the absolute beginners in computer programming to code easily. He lives in Chatillon, near Paris.

Acknowledgments

Foremost, I would like to express my sincere gratitude to my family, my wife Genevieve and my son Adan for the continuous support in my everyday life, for their patience, motivation, enthusiasm. Besides my family, I would like to thank my friends and colleagues: Prof. Jule Villepreux, Hugo D. and Dr. James Rivera, for their encouragement, insightful comments, and hard questions. I thank my fellow labmates: Gang Yu, Ting Fan, Djibrilla Diallo, Juan Sanchez, for the stimulating discussions, for the sleepless nights we were working together before deadlines, and for all the fun we have had. Last but not least, I would like to thank my parents Guy Bell and Ezra Bell, for giving birth to me at the first place and supporting me spiritually throughout my life

Thanks for reading! Please add a short review and let us know what you thought!

Daniel Bell

www.guzzlermedia.com